AN AMERICAN | ANNUAL OF CHRISTMAS LITERATURE AND ART

Christmas

EDITED BY RANDOLPH E. HAUGAN · VOLUME TWENTY

AUGSBURG PUBLISHING HOUSE · PUBLISHERS · MINNEAPOLIS

OPPOSITE PAGE

The Nativity
by Regina Swedenborg

Table of Contents

VOLUME TWENTY   SECOND EDITION   MCML

The Christmas Gospel

Christmas Articles and Stories

Christmas Poetry

Christmas Art and Photography

Christmas Music

Christmas Illustrators

Stryker Ingerman   Sada Jones   Lee Mero   Frank Kofron   David Workman
John L. Ellinghoe   Regina Swedenborg   Garnet Hazard

Acknowledgments

Newman Press	14	Werner Söderström	55
Viking Press	14	Schott & Co., Ltd.	56
A. Pedrett	15	B. H. Smit	56
Metropolitan Museum	16, 17	Hug & Co.	57
Smithsonian Institution	17	Elkan-Vogel Co.	57
L.M.A. Roy	18-21	Felician Sisters	58
Three Lions, Inc.	22-25	Ellertson-Burgess	69-71

THE CHRISTMAS STORY

Illustrated by Stryker Ingerman

SAINT LUKE
Chapter 2 · Verses 1 through 17

AND it came to pass in those days, that there went out a decree from Cæsar Augustus, that all the world should be taxed. (And this taxing was first made when Cyrenius was governor of Syria.) And all went to be taxed, every one into his own city. ✝ ✝ ✝ ❋ And Joseph also went up from Galilee, out of the city of Nazareth, into Judæa, unto the city of David, which is called Bethlehem; (because he was of the house and lineage of David:) to be taxed with Mary his espoused wife, being great with child. ✝ ✝ ✝ ✝ ✝ ❋ And so it was, that, while they were there, the days were accomplished that she should be delivered. And she brought forth her firstborn son, and wrapped him in swaddling clothes, and laid him in a manger; because there was no room for them in the inn. ✝ ✝ ❋ And there were in the same country shepherds abiding in the field, keeping watch over their flock by night. ✝ ✝ ✝ ✝ ✝ ✝ ❋ And, lo, the angel of the Lord came upon them, and the glory of the Lord shone round about them: and they were sore afraid. ✝ ✝ ❋ And the angel said unto them, Fear not: for, behold, I bring you good tidings of great joy, which shall be to all people. For unto you is born this day in the city of David a Saviour, which is Christ the Lord. ✝ ✝ ✝ ✝ ✝ ✝ ✝ ❋ And this shall be a sign unto you; ♦ ♦ ♦ ♦ Ye shall find the babe wrapped in swaddling clothes, lying in a manger. ✝ ✝ ✝ ✝ ✝ ❋ And suddenly there was with the angel a multitude of the heavenly host praising God, and saying, ♦ ♦ ♦ ♦ ♦ ♦ Glory to God in the highest, and on earth peace, good will toward men. ✝ ✝ ✝ ❋ And it came to pass, as the angels were gone away from them into heaven, the shepherds said one to another, ♦ ♦ ♦ ♦ Let us now go even unto Bethlehem, and see this thing which is come to pass, which the Lord hath made known unto us. ✝ ✝ ✝ ✝ ✝ ✝ ✝ ✝ ✝ ❋ And they came with haste, and found Mary, and Joseph, and the babe lying in a manger. And when they had seen it, they made known abroad the saying which was told them concerning this child. ❧ ❧ ❧ ❧ ❧ ❧ ❧ ❧ ❧ ❧ ❧

Glory ···to ·· God ···in ···the ···highest

...and...on...earth...peace,

good...will...toward...men.

SAINT MATTHEW
Chapter 2 ⋯⋯ Verses 1 through 13

NOW when Jesus was born in Bethlehem of Judæa in the days of Herod the king, behold, there came wise men from the east to Jerusalem, saying, Where is he that is born King of the Jews? for we have seen his star in the east, and are come to worship him. ✝ ✝ ✝ ✝ ✝ ✝ ✝ ✝ ✝ ✝
❋ When Herod the king had heard these things, he was troubled, and all Jerusalem with him. And when he had gathered all the chief priests and scribes of the people together, he demanded of them where Christ should be born. ✝ ✝ ✝
❋ And they said unto him, In Bethlehem of Judæa: for thus it is written by the prophet, And thou Bethlehem, in the land of Juda, art not the least among the princes of Juda: for out of thee shall come a Governor, that shall rule my people Israel. ✝ ✝ ✝ ✝ ✝ ✝ ✝
❋ Then Herod, when he had privily called the wise men, inquired of them diligently what time the star appeared. ✝ ✝ ✝ ✝ ✝ ✝ ✝
❋ And he sent them to Bethlehem, and said, Go and search diligently for the young child; and when ye have found him, bring me word again, that I may come and worship him also. ✝ ✝ ✝ ✝ ✝ ✝
❋ When they had heard the king, they departed; and, lo, the star, which they saw in the east, went before them, till it came and stood over where the young child was. When they saw the star, they rejoiced with exceeding great joy.
❋ And when they were come into the house, they saw the young child with Mary his mother, and fell down, and worshipped him: and when they had opened their treasures, they presented unto him gifts; gold, and frankincense, and myrrh. ✝ ✝ ✝ ✝ ✝ ✝ ✝
❋ And being warned of God in a dream that they should not return to Herod, they departed into their own country another way. ✝ ✝
❋ And when they were departed, behold, the angel of the Lord appeareth to Joseph in a dream, saying, ⋯⋯ Arise, and take the young child and his mother, and flee into Egypt, and be thou there until I bring thee word: for Herod will seek the young child to destroy him. ᪥ ᪥ ᪥ ᪥ ᪥ ᪥ ᪥ ᪥

Gold, ... and Frankincense, and Myrrh

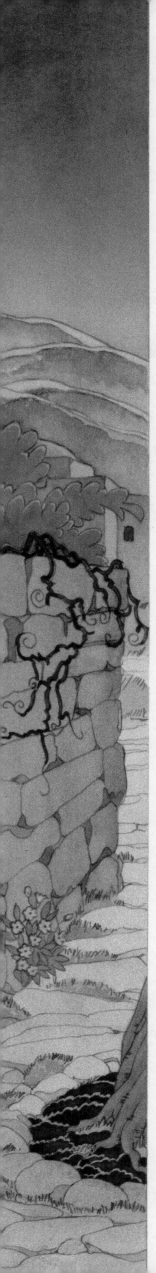

SAINT ✛ ✛ ✛ MATTHEW

Chapter 2 · Verses 14 · 15 ·· and 19 through 23

WHEN he arose, he took the young child and his mother by night, and departed into Egypt: And was there until the death of Herod: that it might be fulfilled which was spoken of the Lord by the prophet, saying, ♦ ♦ ♦ Out of Egypt have I called my son. ♦ ♦ But when Herod was dead, behold, an angel of the Lord appeareth in a dream to Joseph in Egypt, saying, Arise, and take the young child and his mother, and go into the land of Israel: for they are dead which sought the young child's life. And he arose, and took the young child and his mother, and came into the land of Israel. ✛ ✛ ✾ But when he heard that Archelaus did reign in Judæa in the room of his father Herod, he was afraid to go thither: notwithstanding, being warned of God in a dream, he turned aside into the parts of Galilee: ✛ ✛ ✛ ✛ ✛ ✛ ✛ ✾ And he came and dwelt in a city called Nazareth: that it might be fulfilled which was spoken by the prophets, He shall be called a Nazarene. ⟡⟡⟡⟡⟡⟡⟡

The Prince of Peace

(Isaiah 9:6)

"Unto us a child is born,
Unto us a son is given,"
A child of earth for a brief while,
For eternity, a son of heaven.

"And the government," so we are told,
"Shall be upon him," and His name
Is "Wonderful" and "Counsellor,"
And that beneath a star's clear flame
Would be revealed the "mighty God,"
The long awaited "Prince of Peace,"
The "everlasting Father".....Lord,
We pray Thee, bid men's doubtings cease.

May faith that wavered in the dark
Take fire from that holy star;
May nations turn as one to seek
The Prince of Peace, and may mad war
Be done forever from the earth;
May hatred, like a storm, be spent,
And may men move in unison
Under His righteous government.

Grace Noll Crowell

★

Poems for CHRISTMAS

Little Jesus
BY FRANCIS THOMPSON

Little Jesus, wast Thou shy
Once, and just so small as I?
And what did it feel like to be
Out of Heaven, and just like me?
Didst Thou sometimes think of *there,*
And ask where all the angels were?
I should think that I would cry
For my house all made of sky;
I would look about the air,
And wonder where my angels were;
And at waking 'twould distress me—
Not an angel there to dress me!
Hadst Thou ever any toys,
Like us little girls and boys?
And didst Thou play in Heaven with all
The angels that were not too tall,
With stars for marbles? Did the things
Play *Can you see me?* through their wings?
And did Thy Mother let Thee spoil
Thy robes, with playing on *our* soil?
How nice to have them always new
In heaven, because 'twas quite clean blue!

Didst Thou kneel at night to pray,
And didst Thou join Thy hands, this way?
And did they tire sometimes, being young,
And make the prayer seem very long?
And dost Thou like it best, that we
Should join our hands to pray to Thee?
I used to think, before I knew,
The prayer not said unless we do.
And did Thy Mother at the night
Kiss Thee, and fold the clothes in right?
And didst Thou feel quite good in bed,
Kissed, and sweet, and thy prayers said?

Thou canst not have forgotten all
That it feels like to be small:
And Thou know'st I cannot pray
To Thee in my father's way—
When Thou wast so little, say,
Couldst Thou talk Thy Father's way?—

So a little Child, come down
And hear a child's tongue like Thy own;
Take me by the hand and walk,
And listen to my baby-talk.
To Thy Father show my prayer
(He will look, Thou art so fair),
And say: "O Father, I, Thy Son,
Bring the prayer of a little one."

And He will smile, that children's tongue
Has not changed since Thou wast young!

From THE COLLECTED WORKS
OF FRANCIS THOMPSON
Reprinted by permission of
The Newman Press, Westminster, Maryland

Christmas Morning
BY ELIZABETH MADOX ROBERTS

If Bethlehem were here today,
Or this were very long ago,
There wouldn't be a winter time
Nor any cold or snow.

I'd run out through the garden gate,
And go down along the pasture walk;
And off beside the cattle barns
I'd hear a kind of gentle talk.

I'd move the heavy iron chain
And pull away the wooden pin;
I'd push the door a little bit
And tiptoe very softly in.

The pigeons and the yellow hens
And all the cows would stand away;
Their eyes would open wide to see
A lady in the manger hay,

If this were very long ago
And Bethlehem were here today.

And Mother held my hand and smiled—
I mean the lady would—and she
Would take the woolly blankets off
Her little boy so I could see.

His shut-up eyes would be asleep,
And he would look like our John,
And he would be all crumpled too,
And have a pinkish color on.

I'd watch his breath go in and out.
His little clothes would all be white.
I'd slip my finger in his hand
To feel how he could hold it tight.

And she would smile and say, "Take care,"
The mother, Mary, would, "Take care";
And I would kiss his little hand
And touch his hair.

While Mary put the blankets back
The gentle talk would soon begin.
And when I'd tiptoe softly out
I'd meet the wise men going in.

From UNDER THE TREE
by Elizabeth Madox Roberts
Copyright 1922 by B. W. Huebsch, Inc.
Copyright 1950 by Ivor S. Roberts
Reprinted by permission of
The Viking Press, Inc., New York

Switzerland in December
© Photo by A. Pedrett

Candles for Christmas

BY JEAN LOUISE SMITH

CLOSE to the heart of Christmas are its traditions: candles in the windows to light the coming of the Christ-Child on Christmas eve; the Christmas candle-light service; candles on the Christmas tree. It is difficult to imagine Christmas without these customs and the many other ceremonies that involve the use of candles.

Long before the world knew Christ, man associated the light of the candle with spiritual longings. The Old Testament refers frequently to the candle as a symbol of spiritual light. In Psalm 18:28 we read, "For thou wilt light my candle: the Lord my God will enlighten my darkness."

In the beginnings of civilization man came to guard the flame which he discovered he could laboriously make by the friction of sticks or flint. He fashioned crude torches from resin-soaked rushes or from lamps that were simply scooped-out knots of resinous trees. The light of these feeble lamps lengthened his days so that he might further pursue his labor and his search for knowledge.

The first candles were probably used by the Romans to burn before the altars of their gods, to light their great banquet rooms, and to make glorious and dazzling their magnificent pageants and court settings. These first candles were of two kinds: torchlike

A. *Candlestick and rush-light holder, made of iron. Pennsylvania, early 18th century.*

B. *Stand for rush-light, made of iron. American, late 17th century.*

C. *Candlestick, made of pewter. English, 17th century.*

D. *Betty lamp, made of iron. American, 17th century.*

E. *Hanging candlestick, made of iron. New England, 17th or 18th century.*

PHOTOGRAPH ACKNOWLEDGMENTS: A-I from the Metropolitan Museum of Art; J, K, L from the Smithsonian Institution; 1-18 from *The Candle Book* by L. M. A. Roy; 19-31 from George Pickow, Three Lions, Inc.

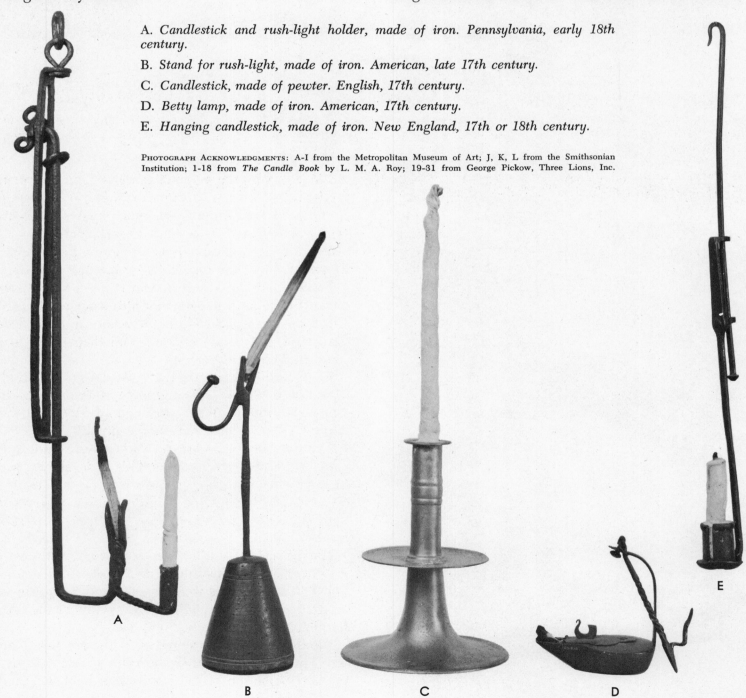

A   B   C   D   E

F   G   H   I

F. *A round tin lantern, perforated to let the candlelight through. American, late 18th century.*

G. *A six-sided tin lantern with glass sides. This type of lantern gave a good light. American, late 18th century.*

H. *Square tin lantern, punched at sides and top. Lanterns were made by the local tinsmith. American, 18th century.*

I. *A more elaborately designed tin lantern. Some of these were quite striking in design. American, late 18th century.*

J. *Three-tube candle-mold*

K. *Six-tube candle-mold*

L. *Eight-tube candle-mold*

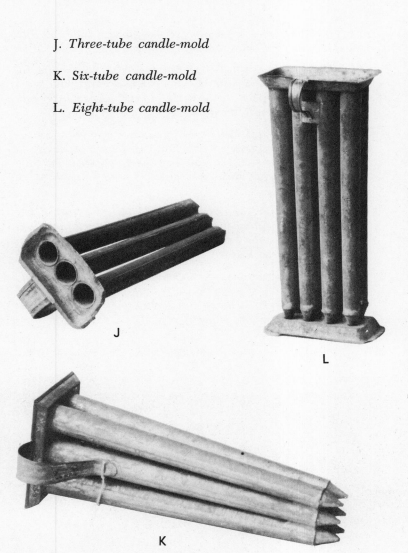

J

L

K

with a fibrous wick made of papyrus, and wax or tallow candles, also with papyrus wicks. While pagan Rome used the candle for its merry-making, the martyr-Christian used it to light the catacombs.

The Christians were quick to adopt the candle as a symbol that was especially adaptable to their beliefs. Had not Christ referred to Himself as the Light of the World, and had He not also asserted that each Christian was a light? Thus, it was only natural that Christians should place candles on their altars to remind them of this teaching.

The Middle Ages were the great days of the candle. Made of tallow, by the dipping process, the candle was widely used for light throughout Medieval times and on up until the nineteenth century.

For the Medieval church, tradition demanded that candles be made of beeswax. This idea had its origin in the belief that bees came to earth directly from heaven. Throughout the Middle Ages it was a common practice to keep swarms of bees at religious establishments.

Candlemas Day, still observed in some churches on February 2, was instituted in the eleventh century. On that day candles were blessed and Scripture was read describing the candle as the symbol of the Christian's love for the indwelling Christ.

Candlesticks, too, originated in the Medieval period. These were often beautifully ornate. A sharp pricket at the top of the candlestick held the candle

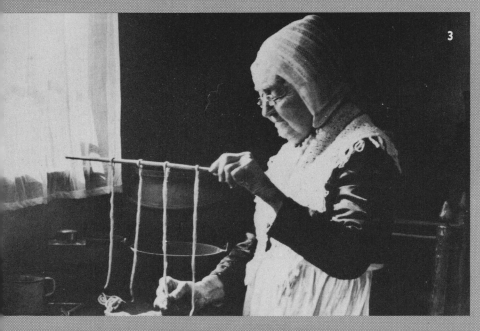

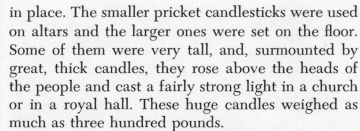

in place. The smaller pricket candlesticks were used on altars and the larger ones were set on the floor. Some of them were very tall, and, surmounted by great, thick candles, they rose above the heads of the people and cast a fairly strong light in a church or in a royal hall. These huge candles weighed as much as three hundred pounds.

Most of the people of that day made their own candles, but there are references to a candle guild in the thirteenth century, showing that itinerant craftsmen made candles. One of the oldest firms of candlemakers in England has been conducting its business on the same spot since Tudor days. In this place, candles are made by hand today in almost exactly the same way that they were made four hundred years ago when much of England's population was living in mud-and-wattle huts.

Throughout these early days, when the candle was a chief source of light, certain customs came to be associated with Christmas. Many of these lovely traditions still persist today. The custom of putting lighted candles on the Christmas tree came from Martin Luther's time and the idea of lights on the tree is still cherished though electricity has replaced candlelight. In one of Albert Schweitzer's early books he tells of a Christmas Day in a steam-

(1) *The first step in making hand-dipped candles is to wind strips of wicking around a board.*

(2) *The wicking is then cut at one edge of the board, making each wick nine inches long when hung double on candle rods, which are about eighteen inches long and a quarter of an inch in diameter.*

(3) *After being inserted on the rods, about two and one-half inches apart, four to a rod, the wicks are twisted and coated with the melted tallow, which is applied with the fingers. This leaves the wicks straight and firm when the tallow hardens.*

(4) *Strained tallow has been poured into a kettle of hot water. As this melted tallow rises to the surface the wicks are lowered into the kettle until the tips of the wicks touch the bottom of the kettle.*

(5) *This picture shows the wicks after the first dipping. The rods holding the wicks are resting on two slat-backed chairs. The tallow is being drained in preparation for the many dippings which will follow.*

Photographs 1-18 are reproduced from *The Candle Book* by L. M. A. Roy, whose mother

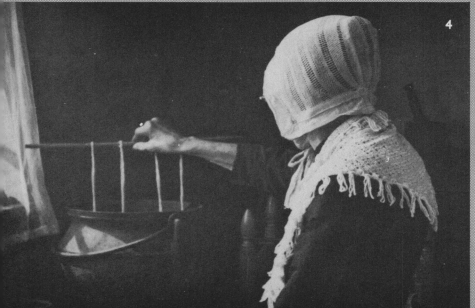

ing African jungle when a dying man begged for a Christmas tree with candles on it.

Every family in Ireland is said to have a candle in the home as a symbol of faith, to welcome the Lord and to invite strangers.

Each Croatian child is given a candle on Christmas Eve and at midnight he lights it from his father's large candle, and as the flame bursts forth he exclaims, "Christ is born!"

In Italy, where St. Francis originated the crèche, a Christmas candle is kept burning in front of each crèche during the Christmas season.

The Christmas candle is placed over the door of each Spanish home, and in Swedish art, St. Lucia, or St. Lucy, is sometimes pictured wearing candles in her hair. Her feast day, December 13, is a forerunner of the Christmas season.

A beautiful scene is enacted in Bulgaria on Christmas Eve when each peasant takes a lighted candle and goes out to the barn to awaken each animal with the greeting, "The Child is born and blesses you tonight."

A pot of incense is then held under the nose of the animal for a moment. Every peasant and each member of his family carries a lighted candle on his way to church. Among the hills and valleys one

(6) *Each time the wicks are dipped, a layer of tallow is deposited and the candles gradually assume the desired size. When the process has been repeated from twelve to fifteen times, the bottom end of the candle will be about three-quarters of an inch in diameter.*

(7) *The roughness formed by the melted tallow as it hardens is removed by scraping with a knife.*

(8) *In this cylindrical tin box, candles may be stored a few at a time to be handy when needed. The box is usually hung near the fireplace so that the lighters can be lighted directly from the fire.*

(9) *The snuffer is used to trim off the hardened carbonized wicks of the candle. Considerable experience is necessary to succeed in snuffing a candle without extinguishing the flame.*

(10) *A small conical metal tube is placed over the candle flame to extinguish it. Some extinguishers have wooden handles, while others are fastened to the candlesticks by small chains so that they will always be handy.*

was photographed while actually making the candles, not just posing for the pictures.

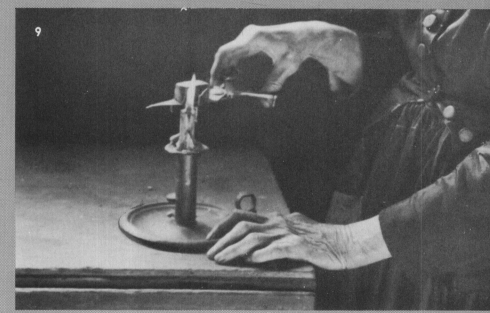

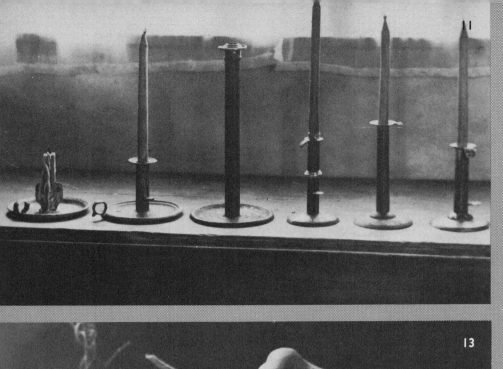

(11) *Candlesticks, of various sizes and shapes, are made of brass, silver, wood, pewter, glass, iron, or tin. Of the tin candlesticks shown the three at the right have lips so that they may be hung from slat-backed chairs. The two at the left have handles so that they may be carried from room to room.*

(13) *Each paper strip is wrapped spirally around a knitting needle to make spills or candle lighters.*

(12) *Lighters or spills are made so that candles can be lighted from the fireplace. They consist of newspaper cut into strips about two feet long and one and one-half inches wide.*

(14) *When the entire strip has been wound on the needle, the needle is withdrawn, and the end of the paper is folded and pinched tightly to keep it from unwinding.*

can see the bobbing, flickering lights of hundreds of candles.

In America's "Christmas City," as Bethlehem, Pennsylvania, is called, much of the Christmas celebration centers around candles. A trombone serenade, played from the steeple of the Moravian Church, ushers in the celebration on the afternoon before Christmas. At a special service on Christmas Eve huge trays laden with lighted wax tapers are distributed to members of the congregation as they sing, "Behold, a great, a heavenly light, from Bethlehem's manger shining bright." The great church is soon aglow with the light of hundreds of candles.

Curiously enough, many of the candles used at Christmas in Bethlehem, Pennsylvania, are made in Simon Rau's Drugstore, the oldest apothecary shop in America. There, in molds the same size as those

used by the original Moravian settlers, the proprietor and his wife cast beeswax candles.

The candle holds a unique place in American history. Early settlers had a way of scheduling an event such as prayer meeting by announcing that it was to be held at "early candlelight." That set the time as late afternoon or early evening when it was customary to light the candles after the chores had been done and people were free to leave their household duties for an hour or two. Some of America's most historic events took place by candlelight. The signing of the Declaration of Independence and the first reception in the White House in 1809, which was held by the light of a thousand candles, are two of the most memorable events.

In the days of the colonists, fat was very scarce and candles were imported from England. Because this

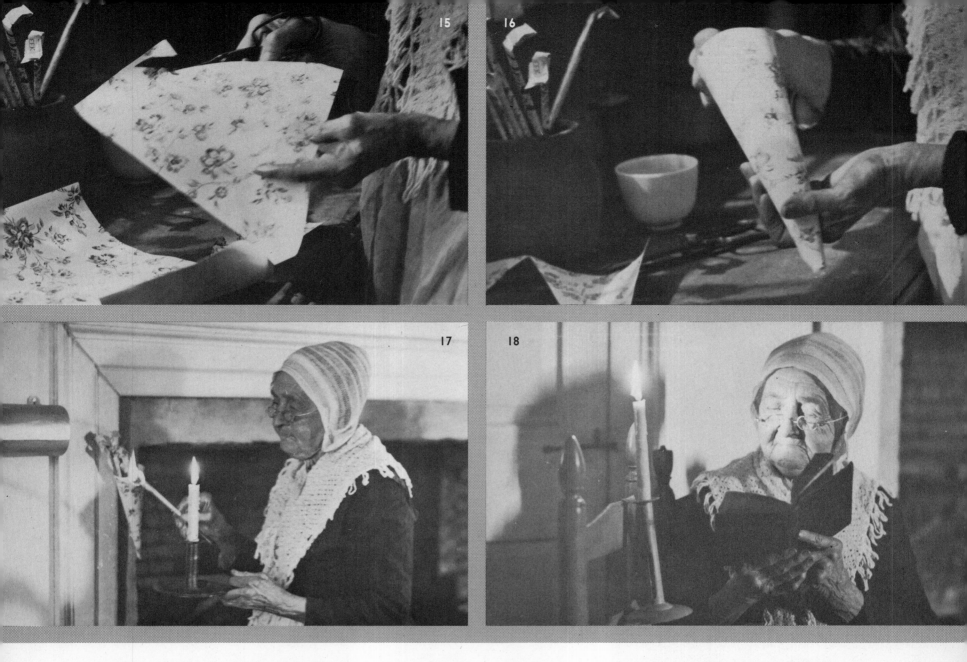

(15) *Holders for the lighters are generally made of heavy decorative paper, such as wallpaper. A piece of suitable paper is cut in the proper shape as shown to form a cornucopia about seven inches long.*

(17) *Here we see a candle being lighted by one of the lighters taken from the well-supplied container which hangs beside the fireplace.*

(16) *Paste is spread along one of the edges and the paper is rolled into the proper shape. A paper loop is then attached to the open end of the container so that it may be hung near the fireplace.*

(18) *The woman of a hundred years ago had little time for reading. But by the light of a hand-dipped candle she was also able to do her mending or plan designs for rag rugs.*

type of lighting was a luxury, the pine torch, commonly used by the Indians, was substituted. Other crude lights were the so-called "candlewood," made from strips of pine wood filled with pitch, and the "rushlight," which was a stripped rush with the pith dipped in grease.

It was always important to keep the flame burning, for if the fire went out it would be necessary to run to a neighbor to borrow a few precious coals in an iron kettle. It took from two minutes to a half-hour to strike a spark by rubbing flint against steel. That spark was then transmitted to dry tinder, such as rotten apple wood or charred rags, and from there to a strip of wood called "spunk." From the spunk it was carried to the candle by a paper lighter called a "spill" made from twisted newspaper. However, when matches were introduced from France in 1827, the

time and effort of making a flame were shortened considerably.

Early American candle-holders are, for the most part, quite simple, since these settlers had little spare time to embellish the arts and crafts. They fashioned these holders from pewter, tin, or wood, making a simple saucer-like arrangement with a handle at the side. A sliding type of candlestick was also developed which had a little knob at the side that could be turned to move the candle higher.

The colonists also made lanterns of sheet iron or tin. The sides of these lanterns were either punched with holes to allow the candlelight to go through, or they were made of glass.

Wall sconces were also used and some of the loveliest of these were made by the Pennsylvania Dutch. These sconces looked like round tin plates, slightly

(19) *In Cape Cod, Massachusetts, where Pilgrim fathers lit the first candles in America, at the shops of the Colonial Candle Company, one of the few concerns that still make candles by the old Early American process of hand-dipping, the long, tapering candles, like pipes of an organ, are suspended from the ceiling as a girl inspects them from butt to tip to see that they are flawless.*

(20) *Large slabs of tallow, frequently the by-product of petroleum refineries, arrive at the candle workshop where they are stacked in a cool underground storage room. In making certain types of candles for religious purposes, it is often necessary to resort to a beeswax base rather than using tallow.*

(21) *The slabs of tallow are melted in a steam-jacketed cauldron. An expert tests the batch periodically for proper consistency before it is drained into dipping vats. If the batch is to be colored, it is done here. Usually color is applied only to the surface, since candles with uncolored interiors burn better.*

(22) *To make certain that each batch is of the same color, the chandler is pouring a sample through the air to cool. When this sample hardens, it will give an indication of the final color, which is often quite different from the color of tallow in liquid form. In his hand the chandler holds some cooled wax.*

(23) *Stringing the wicks for the candles is done on a special frame which will then be dipped into the wax, thus coating many wicks at a time. Such multiple devices for dipping were in use as long ago as the 17th century. Wicks of tightly twisted cotton are most effective, and burn with a steady, clear, white light.*

(24) *From a large revolving drum (upper left) on which are suspended groups of candles-to-be, this woman selects a group at a time, dips it into the hot tallow wax, and returns it to the drum. By the time the dipped candles return to her they are cool and hard, ready for another dipping. About thirty-six dippings are required for an average candle.*

(25) *After the last dipping has been completed, the candles are ready. The cross-section of a candle will reveal the concentric rings resulting from the various dippings. These candles will burn longer and more evenly than candles which have been molded. They are also smoother and have no mold or cutting marks. The uneven excess at the bottom of the candles will be snipped off.*

(26) *The bases or butts of the candles are then inserted into an electrically heated well, which smooths them off to size so that they will fit standard size sockets in candlesticks.*

(27) *Very large candles, which will later be finished by hand, are made in can-like molds into which wicks have been suspended from small sticks. The cans will then be filled with molten wax.*

(28) *Each mold can is then passed through an electrically heated ring which softens the wax along the can's inner surface. This loosens the molded candle, which may then easily be pulled out by the wick with the aid of a pair of pliers.*

(29) *To enhance their contribution to the Christmas season, some of the larger candles are given a polka-dot decoration with the aid of an ingeniously simple little dauber. These monster candles can burn for as long a period as an entire week.*

(30) *Large snowball candles, removed from heavy cast-iron molds, float in water to harden. It requires patience to fill these molds, for as soon as the initial pouring cools, it shrinks and must be supplemented with more wax. This must be repeated several times, until the mold will hold no more.*

(31) *Very popular for the Yuletide is the bayberry candle, whose berry content replaces tallow as a base. The bayberry pictured, when converted into wax candles, will make the latter burn with a pleasant woodsy scent. The candle has a natural green-tan color and is supposed to bring good will and happiness.*

concave, and were often covered with small mirrors for reflection. Another type of candle-holder had a lip at the top by which it could be fastened to the back of a slat-back chair.

For the most part during the days of the early settlers, candles were made by dipping the wicks into bear's grease or deer suet. A big caldron, partially filled with water, was hung over the fire. When the fat, which had been added to it, melted, it rose to the surface.

The rush wicks, suspended vertically from a stick, were then dipped into the fat. This rod or stick was hung from the rungs of a ladder or from two sticks which had been laid horizontally across the backs of two chairs. The wicks were allowed to remain hanging until the wax hardened. Then they were dipped again, hardened, re-dipped, and so on, until enough fat adhered to the wick to make a candle of proper thickness. All of this took time and patience from a life already too full of household duties.

Candles were also made in wooden or tin molds of various sizes, depending on the number of candles they would hold at one time—any amount from two to seventy.

Wicks were made of rough hemp or loosely-spun cotton, and were cut long enough to pass through the mold and allow for knotting. The wicks were threaded through the bottom of the molds, where they were tied so that they would stay in place. At the top of the mold the wicks were pulled taut and tied to small wooden rods.

The strained, hot tallow was then poured into the molds, which were put in a cold place where the tallow could harden. When the candles were ready to be removed from the molds, the knots at the bottom were cut and the mold was submerged in a kettle of hot water long enough to allow the hardened tallow to soften a little next to the tin. Each candle was then drawn out of the mold by pulling on the little wooden rods that held the top of the wick.

Bayberry was sometimes used instead of grease because it was not greasy and was impervious to heat. The fruit of the berry was boiled in a copper or brass kettle with water and then skimmed until the fat became a lovely, soft, transparent green semi-solid. Bayberry candles gave off a delicate, woodsy fragrance. It took a great many berries to yield a small amount of wax.

Candle-holders, snuffers, and extinguishers were all necessary accessories for candle-light. The snuffer was needed to trim the wicks which lacked air space required for proper oxidation.

By 1825 the plaited wick was invented. In this type of wick the burned tip of the wick turned over automatically, exposing it to the air, thus making it self-snuffing. Before the braided wick was perfected, a small straw of rye or oats was sometimes placed next to the wick to give the necessary air space.

This method of candle-making was long and laborious compared to the modern process, which utilizes machinery that speeds up the procedure. But the basic principles are the same as they were in the old days and candles made in a modern factory are either dipped or molded.

Modern candles are made from paraffin wax, fatty acids, or scale wax. Large cakes of wax are first reduced to liquid in huge vats. Wicks are machine-braided and then pickled in a solution of boracic acid and niter, or sal ammoniac, which keeps the wick from burning too fast.

To make dipped candles the wicks are hung in sets of twelve or more from large revolving racks, like those shown on page 24 (illustration 24). These racks turn slowly and as each set of wicks comes to position over a vat of melted wax it is dipped. Fans or air from open windows cools the wax and by the time a set reaches the vat again, the previous dipping has hardened enough to allow another dipping.

Candles build up slowly at the first dippings and then toward the finish they build up more rapidly. They are made thicker at the bottom and tapered at the top by means of a certain number of partial dippings. Color is added by dipping the candles in dye and then once in water to give them a gloss. The base is shaped by submerging the butt in warm wax or a hot die until the right amount of wax has melted away from the candle. Quick fingers trim the wicks at the top and bottom and the candles are ready for packaging.

Molded candles are cheaper to make than those which are dipped. Molding machines are of various sizes, and from 80 to 512 candles can be made at one time and two or three "charges" can be made in one hour. The wick is threaded up through the bottom of each cylindrically-shaped mold. The melted wax is then poured into the molds and allowed to remain until sufficiently hard. Water circulation coils, built into the molding machine, cool the candles gradually. They are then expelled by pistons into wooden receiving racks, the wicks are trimmed, and the candles are finished.

More candles are sold today than has been the case for many years. It is estimated that half the annual output goes to the religious market, since Catholics, Protestants, and Jews all use candles in their services and ceremonies.

For the Christian the candle is a constant reminder of the words of Jesus: "Ye are the light of the world." From Christ comes a light which must never be hid, but which is intended to shine forth brightly through us. As long as men have faith in God, they will cherish the symbol of the candle.

Adoration of the Magi

Albrecht Dürer

1471-1528

BY ADALBERT RAPHAEL KRETZMANN

IN THE last picture painted by Albrecht Dürer, there is a magnificent summing up of the knowledge and the devotion of a lifetime in the presentation of "The Four Apostles." In presenting this to the governors of Nürnberg in 1526, two years before his death, Dürer said, "For a long time I have intended to present to you, as a humble remembrance, some picture of mine, but I have been prevented by the imperfection of my works. Now, however, I have finished a picture on which I have bestowed more trou-

ble than on any other painting, and I consider none more worthy to keep it than the governors of my native town." Virtually every recognized authority acclaims this picture one of the greatest sixteenth century contributions to Christian art. The painting is in two panels, one representing John and Peter, the other Paul and Mark. Beneath the figures Dürer had added an inscription stating that he presented "The Four Apostles" to the town "as a warning against evil and falsehood, and as an eternal admonition

27

Munich, Alte Pinakothek

Self-Portrait
at Age 29

Oil on wood, 1500

Munich, Alte Pinakothek

The Four Apostles
John, Peter, Mark, and Paul

Oil on wood, 1526

to truth, uprightness, sincerity and Christian love."

Albrecht Dürer was a remarkable man. Born in Nürnberg on May 21, 1471, he was the third of eighteen children. We learn most about his attitude toward his family from what he has to say about them, especially about his parents. Very early in life he wrote some splendid things in tribute to his father who was an expert goldsmith. Four years before his father's death this tribute is recorded, "My dear father passed his life in great toil, in difficult and arduous labor, having only what he earned by his handiwork to support his family. He brought up his children to love God and to act honorably toward all men. He experienced many troubles and reverses, but he was patient and gentle, at peace with the world and full of gratitude to his Maker."

His mother died in 1514. Her thin, tired face is known best of all from the loving way in which he drew her features shortly before her death. Her loss meant much to him and his tribute to her is worthy of remembering, "She kept us, my brothers and myself, with great care from all sin, and on my coming or going it was her habit to say, 'Christ bless thee.' I cannot praise enough her good works, the kindness and charity she showed to all."

One sad chapter in his life seems to have been his marriage to *Agnes Frey*. She was a very good-looking woman and brought with her a considerable dowry, but from the accounts written by a life-long friend of the artist, she was a skin-flint and a scold, second only to the wife of Socrates. His friend wrote, "He called her *meine Agnes* and made many beautiful drawings and paintings of her and took her with him to the Netherlands where she made everybody sit up and take notice, for she was something for sore eyes in her fine clothes, but, to tell the truth, Agnes worried Albrecht into his grave. I don't deny that she was virtuous and pious, but I, for my part, would prefer a roguish woman who behaved in a free way to such a nagging, suspicious sourface."

Some of Dürer's happiest days were spent in Venice, where he worked in closest proximity to the painter *Giovanni Bellini*. He must have been treated in a princely way, and yet he felt himself drawn back to his homeland. His brief encounter with the Italian artists left some impression upon them, for under his open-hearted instruction and sharing of his skill, many of them learned how to use brushes correctly and to bring into their paintings some of the marvelous detail which was Dürer's greatest asset.

Nürnberg carried in its hallowed, ancient walls all the inspiration that an artistic temperament could desire. Even in those early days of Dürer's life the city could look back upon a history of almost five hundred years. On the rock to the north of the town stood the castle in which kings and emperors had found refuge for hundreds of years. The old walls of the city were most of them still standing. They were famous for their ten elaborate gates and for their three hundred and sixty-five bastions named after the calendar days of the year. There was the Eleventh Century royal palace which was the marvel of the age. In this city some of the first terrestrial and celestial globes had been made already at this time, and Dürer's skills were employed to draw globes in considerable detail for *Johann Stabius*. Stabius was court astronomer to the Emperor. These representations show a tremendous technical skill and a brilliant sense of cartography almost completely out of tune with that age.

It was characteristic that he should have deep thoughts about the whole matter of beauty. "What beauty is," Dürer wrote, "I do not know, but it depends upon many things. The artist must inquire widely so that he will have a mind well stored. The beautiful figure he makes then is not to be called wholly his own. It is partly acquired and learned. Nevertheless, the secret feeling of the heart also is manifested in the image and thus a new thing, not in nature, but created, is brought into the world." One might easily read into Dürer's words a statement of esthetics very similar to the most modern credo. The insistence upon the independent and invented quality of the work of art beyond a transcription from nature is especially "up-to-date." Dürer's own works are evidence that with him the observing eye and controlling brain were given more sway than the secret images of the heart. Dürer's is a philosophical and intellectual conception and he was never guilty of the overtones and unreal meanings obtained by the distortions of Tintoretto and El Greco.

His years of training under Michael Wohlgemuth stood him in good stead. The work that his father had given him to do in goldsmithing had strengthened his hands to an almost supernatural beauty. It has been said of his self-portrait at the age of twenty-nine that the hand which holds the fur-trimmed mantle together is one of the most beautiful hands in all painting and draws the comment, "Nothing more beautiful than Dürer's hands could be imagined." This self-portrait, in common with the others, bears a startling resemblance to his pictures of Christ, a resemblance that is not forced nor accidental. Dürer was famous for the beauty of his person and he depicted himself in the light of an ideal he strove to attain. He believed firmly that the kind of life that a man led was reflected in his face and in his looks, and that an artist aspiring to create the Christ-like ideal should live in the utmost purity of spirit. And he practiced what he preached.

Berlin, Kupferstichkabinett *The Holy Family* Pen drawing, 1493

Berlin, Kupferstichkabinett *Portrait of His Mother* Charcoal drawing, 1514

Close to his house was the famous Hauptmarkt of the city and on the opposite side of the Hauptmarkt was the Church of Our Lady. As a small boy he saw them install the lovely clock which has the electors moving around the figure of Charles the Fourth. Familiar to his eyes, too, were the ten towers of St. Sebaldus Church, where, during his middle twenties, he had the opportunity to see Vischer's splendid work on the shrine of St. Sebaldus develop. He was enormously impressed with the patient labors of this man, who took thirteen years to complete the canopy, the sarcophagus, and the statues of the saints around the shrine. In his own church, St. Lorenz, he saw the sixty-five-foot ciborium that had been made with such meticulous care by Kraft, and even in the tiniest part of the detail there was revealed the loving care and devotion of a truly great artist.

Out in the infamous five-cornered tower he saw the perfection of all torture, the Iron Maiden, in which heretics were clamped until the nails or spikes within the iron virgin pierced them through and through. But when the snow came upon the red-tiled roofs, and the great castle built by Frederick the First showed up in its white splendor, then the city became truly the Christmas town. Many were the memories that he held of the holy season when all was joy and peace. There is no record that they dressed the house with a tree, but he speaks of the sweet-smelling garlands that were brought from the hills to make "the house alive with the ever green, ever living spirit of the love of the Christ Child."

In Venice he had evidently seen his first *praecipio*, and tradition has it that he designed two or three of them for churches in and around Nürnberg. One of them, in the Church of Our Lady, is directly attributed to him. Even if none of the things which are traditionally ascribed to Christmas in the life of Albrecht Dürer are true, it is, nevertheless, quite evident from his representations of the Madonna and the Child that this was to him an event of paramount importance and a real manifestation of God's love. His famous pen drawing, "The Holy Family" in a landscape, which is preserved in the Berlin Museum, was done about the year 1493. The virgin is shown as a young and lovely mother with her Child set in the midst of a very elaborate and well designed landscape.

A close study of the head of the "Twelve-Year-Old Jesus," which is found in the Vienna Museum, is an example of the true simplicity which is characteristic or the early period of Dürer's life. The famous study of the "Hands in Adoration," which has been so widely reproduced, was actually done in brush and India ink on paper with a blue prepared surface heightened with white. It was only a preliminary study for the hands of a kneeling apostle in the so-called Heller Altar (1499) and is a masterpiece in itself. In 1511 he did a very faint outline of a draw-

ing for a "Madonna With Two Angels" which is worth considerable study because it was prepared for the Emperor Maximilian's Christmas. In Munich is preserved a page from the printed prayer book of Emperor Maximilian which is decorated with hand drawings by Dürer that show a splendid union of figures. Among the best Christmas pictures by the artist are two pen drawings, one "The Holy Family," preserved in the Vienna Albertina Museum, and the other, "The Virgin Crowned by Angels," which is a sketch for the engraving of 1518. In the same Museum is found the very precious "Adoration of the Kings," which is easily one of the greatest of his drawings, undoubtedly made as a preliminary to a wood cut of the same subject. It is dated 1524 and bears the monogram A D.

In America the most famous Dürers are the "St. Anne with the Virgin and Child" in the Metropolitan Museum in New York, "Portrait of a Young Man" (1504) in Indianapolis, and "Portrait of a Young Man" (1507) in Washington. The Toledo Museum of Art has the "Portrait of Jobst Planckfelt." The Pierpont Morgan library carries the "Adam and Eve" pen and sepia drawing of 1504. In the Bache Collection in New York City is the "Portrait of a Woman" (1506) which carries the initials A D embroidered in the bodice of her dress. The Honolulu Academy of Arts has a copper engraving of "The Great Horse" from 1505.

Dürer is, of course, most famous because of the fact that he was the poor man's artist. As fast as the sheets could be pulled from his wood blocks, they were on sale in the stalls of the city of Nürnberg. Today those pictures of the Large and Small Passion are almost priceless. In those days they were happily—and fortunately—the pride and possession of countless numbers of humble people who graphically saw the life of their Lord and Saviour Jesus Christ in the skilled development of pictures in black and white under the tooling of this great master. Perhaps the spirit of Hans Sachs and the other *Meistersänger* rang out through his prints and etchings.

He died in the midst of his work. Indeed, his last work was a drawing of himself in red chalk. One hand points to a spot on his side and under the drawing are the words, "Where my finger points is the yellow spot, the seat of my illness." He was fifty-seven years old when he died. Of him Goethe wrote, "In truth and nobility, and even in beauty and grace, Dürer, if one really knows him in heart and mind, is equalled only by the very greatest of the Italian masters." Till the end of days his "The Worship of the Holy Trinity" and the "Adoration of the Kings" will rank among the world's great masterpieces, not only because of the perfect technique which shows itself there, but because of religious faith and clear-sightedness which leaves one completely breathless before the miracle of his vision of the love of God and the purpose of God among the children of men.

CHRISTMAS
IN THE CITY

"Once upon a time"

Being the sequel to

CHRISTMAS IN THE COUNTRY

That was the year when Uncle Erik and Aunt Stella got the Thorkelsons to care for the farm while they went "up to the city" to spend the Holidays with John and Clara.

scat!

Illustrations by LEE MERO

They took the 6:17 A.M. "accommodation train"

"fresh fruit, chewin' gum, magazines"

(It "accommodated" freight, livestock and people)

Erik and Stella arrived at the Union Depot, which was even BIGGER than they had imagined!

"A Hack", says Mr Webster, "is a carriage for hire".

An almost endless line of hacks waited to drive folks to their destinations

They got a real thrill, though, when John said they would ride out home in one of the new E-LEC-TRIC CARS -- complete with trailer!

"Faster and more comfortable", he said, as they found seats next to the stove for the two mile ride —

Erik's Telescope grip

ERIK MARTELL WISC.

Yes sir!" said John, "these are going to put horse-cars right out of business!"

Next morning, after the grocer had called for his daily order, everybody left home for a trip downtown, "to go through the stores."

"Just like fairy-land!" exclaimed Stella.

She didn't forget to buy a souvenir coffee spoon for Mrs. Thorkelson.

On the way home the Turkey was bought,

Next day, the wood·box was filled to overflowing

The children had a final rehearsal for the Sunday school program

The Turkey was plucked,

Good things fairly popped from the oven!

Uncle Erik "slicked up" his celluloid collar

And a nice goose was sent over to the parsonage

That evening they went over to the Exposition Building to hear the "Messiah"

And Stella got a chance to observe what the ladies up in the city were wearing

On Christmas Eve, the candles were lighted

As usual, the gifts were "just what everyone wanted!"

Clara ALWAYS stood by with a handy pail of water.

"Except— Erik's jacket seemed a bit large!

CHRISTMAS MORNING the snow-plows were out early to clear the walks.

The family attended service at one of the BIG churches downtown

(a generous gift from his congregation had made the pastor's dream come true)

"Now, my Son, I can see my way to send you to college"

Cream of Tomato soup
celery, olives
pickles
turkey ham
potatoes mashed
escalloped
peas rutabagas
beet pickles
pineapple sherbet
apple mince
cranberry pie
cheese nuts
coffee milk

Clara planned the customary Christmas dinner. Later, other relatives living in the city dropped in to visit with Erik and Stella and so the turkey got a final going over for the evening lunch

Ice-boats made
a pretty picture

The day after Christmas, being a very
nice one for this time of year, John rented
a team and a two-seated sleigh and
took the family on his favorite ride
around the parkways.

The Park was thronged
with skaters

Stella thought
"the Falls" were
"just like fairy-land!"

John "saved up" the most exciting entertainment for the last evening! Then, they went to the neighborhood fire-barn, where, promptly at eight, the fire drill took place. The gong rang, the horses pranced to their places, a fireman slid down the pole and "a pleasant time was had by all!"

the Captain

MASCOT OF COMPANY EIGHT

Erik thought "the dappled grays were just wonderful!"

They didn't want to appear too much like "country cousins" while they were with John and Clara, but on the way home, they talked about:

"How Clara didn't have to pump water"

"Those good, hot chestnuts at five cents a bag"

"The man who lit the gas light with a newfangled device on the end of a stick",

And how he thawed it out with a long iron rod when it froze up!"

"The steaming kettle sign for a tea and coffee store"

"All those pieces of Grandma's china that Erik could mend with that new cement the man sold him!

"How much they enjoyed the Christmas music"

But, after all, it was good to be "HOME AGAIN" when the Thorkelsons met them at the station with the bob-sled!

CANDLES burn at Christmas time, casting their tender glow upon the Holy Child as Mary holds Him close. All nature bows in adoration to the King of Kings.

People of many lands bow down before Him too. Not always are the melodies of their songs the same. Nor are their customs and traditions alike. But they all seek the Star that shone over the stable where Christ was born in Bethlehem. They all bring gifts of gold and frankincense and myrrh. And the message of their songs, whatever the language, is "Glory to God . . . and on earth peace. . . ."

Candles burn at Christmas time, casting their tender glow upon the Holy Child as Mary holds Him close. And nature bows in adoration to the King of Kings.

Text by MELVA ROREM . . . . *Illustrated by* SADA JONES

ENGLAND

THEIR voices, strong and sweet, suddenly break forth outside the door. Lighted candles in the windows, that tell the story of the Christ-Child who wanders the fields and woods and streets at Christmas time, have led them here. For the candle is a symbol of both cheer and compassion. And any wayfarer, too, who seeks warmth and shelter on a winter's night is welcomed in the Christ-Child's name.

So it was in England long ago, and so it is today. In early Britain wandering bards and harpers found their way to castles where their songs of chivalry filled the air. Later, the carolers, or "waits," sang Christmas songs to the accompaniment of the harp and the fiddle and the flageolet. And still today, on city streets and village lanes, the age-old songs ring true and clear.

There is a song for the Yule Log ritual, when garlanded with greens it is triumphantly drawn to the house amid shouts of joy and laughter. Each member of the jolly group sits for a moment on the log, hums a bit of lilting carol, and salutes the log with a kiss—an assurance of good luck until another Christmas comes.

There are songs for Boxing Day, the day after Christmas, when newsboys, mail carriers, and servants go from house to house and receive gifts. There are songs when neighbors gather to taste each family's Yule Cake as it is ceremoni-

GOD REST YOU MER-RY GEN-TLE-MEN, LET NOTH-ING YOU DIS-MAY

ously cut. And legend tells us that the sweetest song of all is heard on Christmas Eve at midnight, when oxen in their stalls kneel in adoration of the Christ-Child, and unseen choristers praise His name.

SWEDEN

DOWN the winding stairway Saint Lucia comes. She wears a long white dress trimmed with gay colors and a red sash, and her halo is a crown of lighted candles at whose base bilberry twigs are intertwined. Pride and joy are singing happy songs in her heart. For has she not been chosen "the prettiest girl in the house"? And yet her pride is graced by humility, for on Saint Lucia's Day, December thirteenth, she who is loveliest of all becomes the servant of all as she goes from room to room in her home at the first cock-crowing, singing the carols of her land and serving hot coffee and cakes to each one she awakens.

The first Saint Lucia, a maiden of the Roman Empire, for whom the day was named, lived long ago in the city of Syracuse on the island of Sicily. As the day approached that should have been her wedding day, the story goes, she gave her dowry to poor Christians whose courage shone like a beacon light in her pagan world. Her defiant fiancé informed officials that Lucia was a Christian, and the Emperor Diocletian condemned her to be burned at the stake. But though the fire was all about her she remained unharmed, until finally her heart was pierced by a sword. The people of Sweden chose to make her their heroine, and through the years they have sung her praise and honored her day.

Although the preparations for the festive holiday begin as early as the first day of December, it is the celebration of Saint Lucia's Day that ushers in the Christmas season. What planning! What cleaning! What baking! The curtains must be fresh and white. The copper must gleam brilliantly. Food must be prepared. Gifts must be made and wrapped and sealed with red sealing wax. And the house must be scoured from top to bottom, for dust, like sinful thoughts, cannot be tolerated during the Holy Season.

Saint Lucia's Day! Festival of lights! Day for beginning the journey to the lowly manger where the Father of Lights lay that first Christmas Morn!

BAVARIA

OH, THE everlasting wonder of the *Tannenbaum!* Last year it could not have been more beautiful, it seemed. But this year its stars, its candles, its silver nuts, and its shining baubles are of matchless beauty. And beneath it our beloved Christmas Crib! Mother trimmed the Tree this afternoon and when the curtains were drawn back, there it stood in all its wondrous enchantment.

Twilight falls, and carols have been sung, and the Christmas supper is over. Then it is that an age-old custom is re-enacted in Bavaria when hundreds of marksmen, *schutzen,* go from their small farms hidden deep in the valleys, up to their beloved mountains. Some of them jour-

O CHRIST-MAS TREE. O CHRIST-MAS TREE, O TREE OF GREEN UN-CHANG-ING

ney three or four hours. Sometimes the wives and daughters of the farmers join them, too, all of them wearing colorful Bavarian costumes and carrying knapsacks of hand mortars, *handboller*. For everyone wishes to have a part in the tumultuous noise which, tradition says, protects the entire countryside from evil or mischievous spirits which wander about on Christmas Eve. Half an hour before midnight the sky is a sea of fire as all guns and hand mortars are fired simultaneously, fireworks are lighted, and bonfires are kindled on the highest mountain peaks. But at midnight when the church bells ring, silence settles over the land, and the merry groups go down to the valley for the Christmas service.

Candles shine from every window to light the *Kristkind* on her way from home to home. She is the messenger of the Infant Jesus, and Bavarian children believe that she brings them their gifts. She wears a white robe. She has golden wings. In her hand she carries a small Christmas Tree. And the crown that she wears on her head was placed there by the Holy Christ.

FRANCE

THE air is filled with sweet Noëls sung to *le petit* Jesus who lies in a manger. And song is mingled with the crunch-crunch of snow beneath wooden sabots and happy shouts and gay voices. For bringing home the Yule Log is a joyous festivity.

Dressed in their holiday attire, the father and oldest son triumphantly lead the way pulling the newly cut log. Mother and the other children, from the oldest daughter to the tiniest son, follow, carrying garlands of fresh greens. And all is happiness and merriment.

In reverent ceremony the log is carried through the doorway by father and son. Three times the room is circled before the log is placed in the fireplace. And the time has come for the log to be lighted with a brand of last year's log. . . . The throat tightens and the heart quickens a bit as the new log takes torch and glows—an emblem of the Light that came to earth when Christ was born.

A moment of tenderness falls. And bells peal out throughout the land as little children light the tri-colored candles of their crèche in honor of the Trinity. Christmas has come!

POLAND

FONDLY they carry their Christmas crib, the *Szokka,* from home to home through village streets. For does it not show their Treasure—the Infant Jesus, adored by Mary, Joseph, and the shepherds? Some of the children carry bright, burning candles. One clutches tightly the hand of a little sister who has perhaps been allowed to go along for the first time. Sometimes a large star in which a candle is burning is carried on top of a pole. But always there are songs. Songs for the Holy Festival of the Star!

After prayers are said on Christmas Eve, and when the first star appears in the evening sky, the Christmas feast begins. Straw is scattered on the floor or under the tablecloth, in remembrance of the stable at Bethlehem, and always a chair is drawn to the table for the Holy Child. Small wafers, *oplatek,* which have been blessed by the church and marked with scenes of the Nativity, are given to everyone. Each one shares his wafer with every other person at the table as a token of friendship and a symbol of peace on earth.

A ringing of the bell after the feast means that the gifts have arrived for the children. Mother Star, who is dressed like an angel in a white robe and veil, distributes the gifts after Father Star, who is a bit to be feared, listens to the children's prayers and catechism.

Legend tells us that on this Holy Night the heavens open and those who have lived pure lives can see the vision of Jacob's ladder. And that animals who were honored by His presence on that first Christmas night are able to tell of wondrous things to be. Quaint and beautiful are the customs of Poland!

NORWAY

THE birds' Christmas Tree! Dear to the hearts of the people of Norway is this custom. A Christmas feast for the animals and birds, since they were present at the Christ-Child's birth in the stable. The cattle are given extra fodder, and all the beasts of the farm are given special care. Even *Julenissen,* the little elf-like creature who is a part of the household all through the year, though he is never seen as he helps with a task here and plays a mischievous trick there, is rewarded on Christmas Eve.

But the birds especially are remembered. . . . In the morning or in early afternoon bits of suet are hung on the snow-laden trees in the garden. And a choice sheaf of grain is tied to a pole near the house. Another may be placed near the gable of the barn, or tied to trees, fences, gateways, and house tops. The birds will have a Christmas dinner indeed!

When twilight falls an old carol for the lighting of the Tree is sung as Mother lights the candles, and Father and the children encircle the Tree singing:

> Then Mother lights the Christmas tree,
> And fills the room with light,
> She says that so the Star shone forth,
> And made the whole world bright.

Then over the land of deep fjords and frozen lakes, snow-clad mountains and fragrant pine-woods, bells from a thousand towers ring out the good news that Christmas has come. For an hour they ring, loudly, clearly, exultantly . . . kling-klang, kling-klang . . . and the darkness of night settles down. But candle lights in windows and lighted Christmas Trees in every home tell that families are reunited for this dearest of seasons, and that joy is everywhere.

AMERICA

T HE new Christmas sled, wonder in the eyes of little
children, mysterious gifts piled high, the glow of
candlelight on faces of loved ones, mistletoe and holly,
poinsettia and winter greens, and families—reunited for
this happiest of days—going to church on Christmas Morn.
. . . This is Christmas in America.

It is not like Christmas in any other land, for it is like Christmas in many lands. As children of other countries became children of America, they brought with them to their churches and homes in a new country rich treasures of custom and tradition. And into the pattern that is now America's Christmas have been woven colorful threads of bits of Christmas from everywhere.

Carols from England, Saint Lucia celebrations from Sweden, the Christmas Tree from Saxony, the Yule Log from France, the Christmas Crib from Poland, the birds' Christmas Tree from Norway.... These, and many more delightful traditions, are now a part of Christmas in America.

BELLS ring at Christmas time throughout the world . . . from great cathedral towers, from belfries of the country church. And men are called in every clime to bow in worship to the Christ of Bethlehem. Bells ring at Christmas time; their song, a carol true, rings loud and clear—"Christ is born!"

Christmas Is Here

JOULU PUU ON RAKENNETTU

Finnish Folk Song

English Version · MRS. EDW. J. ISAAC AND HERMAN E. JORGENSEN

Once a-gain has come our Yule-tide with its ra-di-ant Christmas tree;
Jou-lu puu on ra-ken-net-tu, jou-lu on jo — o-vel — la

Decked with lights, with stars and tin-sel, It is hailed with songs of glee.
Na-mu-si-a ri-pus-tet-tu om-pi kuu-sen ok-sil-la.

2 Round the tree in merry circles
Children play in festive mirth,
And they sing, while lights are gleaming,
Of the blessed Saviour's birth.

3 On this holy eve, Lord Jesus,
When of old God's angels came
To our earth with gladsome tidings,
We do praise Thy holy name.

4 For into this world's deep darkness
Thou didst bring Thy saving light,
That the way to life eternal
We may find through time's dark night.

5 Bless for us, O Christ, our Yuletide,
Give to all true Christmas cheer;
Fill us with Thy Holy Spirit,
Make our faith in Thee sincere.

2 Kuusen pienet kynttiläiset
valaisevat kauniisti.
Ympärillä lapsukaiset
laulelevat sulosti.

3 Kiitos sulle Jeesuksemme,
Kallis Vapahtajamme!
Kun Sä tulit vieraaksemme,
paras joululahjamme.

4 Tullessasi toit sä valon,
lahjat rikkaat, runsahat,
autuuden ja anteeksannon,
kaikki taivaan tavarat.

5 Anna, Jeesus, Henkes hyvän
meidän sydämihimme
viritellä uskon valon!
Siunaa, Jeesus, joulumme!

We are indebted to Werner Soderstrom O/Y, Porvoo, Finland, and to the Finnish Book Concern, Hancock, Michigan, publishers of SÄVELMISTÖ and AAPINEN, for the Finnish carol "Christmas Is Here". Schott & Co. Ltd., London, has given permission to include the carol "Sing Merrily This Happy Day," which is taken from SEVEN CZECHOSLOVAK CAROLS, compiled by Vilem Tausky and Sheila Lennox Robertson. The Dutch carol "The Star of Bethlehem" is reproduced by permission of B. H. Smit, Amsterdam, from the publication KERSTGEFLONKER. "Tomorrow, Children, There'll Be Joy" is a German carol from Kurt Herrmann's Album ES IST EIN ROS' ENTSPRUNGEN, published by Hug & Co., Zurich. "In This Stable" is based on a carol found in the collection 40 NOELS ANCIENS selected by Leon Roques, published by Durand & Cie, Paris, distributed by Elkan-Vogel Co., Philadelphia. The Felician Sisters, Buffalo, New York, have published a collection of carols entitled HEJ KOLEDA, from which we have the carol "Lo! Angel Bands."

Sing Merrily this Happy Day

VESELÉ VÁNOČNÍ HODY

English text-
MARY COCHRANE VOJÁČEK

Czechoslovak Carol
Arrangement- MRS. M.H. HEGGE

mf

Sing merri-ly this hap-py day. Sing, broth-ers, sing this ca-rol gay, Gai-ly sing, the
Ve-se-lé vá-no-čni ho-dy, zpi-vej-te, bra-tři, ko-le-dy o-tom co se

truth a-dorn-ing, That to us on Christmas morn-ing Christ was born. Christ was born. Christ was born.
vsku tku sta-lo, že se li-dem na-ro-di-lo dě-t'a-tko.

ff

The Star of Bethlehem

DE STER VAN BETHLEHEM

Dutch Text· HERRE DE VOS   English Version· GLADYS J. WOGEN   Music· HERRE DE VOS

WISE MEN·

O bright, guiding star, won't you qui-et stand? We've
"Kom ster-re-tje, wil je niet stil-le staan? Wy

trav-eled so far o'er the des-ert sand. A-wait here the morn, For
zyn al zoo lange op reis ge-gaan. We zyn er zoo moe, zoo

wea-ry and worn, We come from the East, a far-off land!
zorglyk aan-toe We ko-men uit't Oosten, hier ver van-daan!

STAR·

2 "Have patience, O Wise Men, for Mary too,
Now knows that her waiting is nearly through.
Come, follow afar
The twinkling star,
For what has been promised will soon come true.'

2 "Neen Koningen, hebt nogeen wyl geduld!
Maria haar dagen zyn haast vervuld!
Komt volgt maar van ver,
De glanzende ster,
Opdat ge uw doel eens bereiken zult."

3 Then came they to Bethlehem, still and old,
As led by the star through the night so cold.
Ne'er twinkled so bright
The star's wondrous light
As Mary the Child gently doth enfold.

4 The star then stood still in the valley bright
Where found they the Christ in the stall that night.
They humbly knelt down
With honor to crown
Our Lord and Redeemer, our Life and Light.

3 Ze kwamen in Beth'lem, de stille stad,
Waarheen hen de sterre gedreven had......
Nooit straalde haar glans
Zoo helder als thans·
Zy wees waar Maria met't Kindje zat.

4 En stil stond de sterre in't stille dal,
Daar vonden zy Jezuke in een stal......
Daar knielden zy neer,
Daar brachten zy eer,
Den Heer die van zonden ons redden zal.

Tomorrow, Children, There'll be Joy

MORGEN, KINDER, WIRDS WAS GEBEN

English Version = OSCAR R. OVERBY

German Folk Tune

Chil-dren, there'll be joy to-mor-row, Thrills that mem-o-ries a-rouse. Gai-e-ty and loud re-joic-ing

Mor-gen, Kin-der, wirds was ge-ben, mor-gen wer-den wir uns freun, welch ein Ju-bel, welch ein Le-ben

Soon will ech-o through our house. Soon the morn-ing lights the way-- We a-wake, it's Christ-mas Day!

wird in un-serm Hau-se sein, ein-mal wer-den wir noch wach, hei-sa, dann ist Weih-nachts-tag!

2

How the living-room will glitter
With the many candles bright,
Fairer than a royal palace
Full of wonder and delight!
You'll remember, I believe,
How it was last Christmas Eve.

3

What a glorious day tomorrow!
New anticipations grow.
Yes, our good and thoughtful parents
Made provision long ago.
Honor unto them we voice,
Lest unworthy we rejoice.

Wie wird dann die Stube glänzen
Von der grossen Lichterzahl,
Schöner als bei frohen Tänzen
Ein geputzter Kronensaal.
Wisst ihr noch, wie voriges Jahr
Es am heilgen Abend war?

3

Welch ein schöner Tag ist morgen!
Neue Freuden hoffen wir,
Unsre guten Eltern sorgen
Lange, lange schon dafür.
O gewiss, wer sie nicht ehrt,
Ist der ganzen Lust nicht wert.

In this Stable

DANS CETTE ÉTABLE

English Version = OSCAR R. OVERBY

Traditional French Carol
Arranged = OSCAR R. OVERBY

2
Great is His glory.
This day His power appears,
Though love reduced Him
To be a child in tears.
Our trembling, conquered foe
And hell confused below
Are fearful at His coming.
They dread His might; they know,
Great is His glory.

3
Lost in the wonder
Of His divinity,
I sense the vastness
Of all His majesty.
And in this babe divine,
In whom delights combine,
I find my Lord, my Master,
And joy to call Him mine--
Lost in the wonder.

4
O boundless sorrow!
A God must suffer pain,
Appease His Father,
That ours may be the gain.
For us He came, He bore
The grief, the burden sore,
That we might share His glory
With Him forevermore.
O boundless sorrow!

3
Sans le connaître,
Dans sa divinité
Je vois paraître
Toute sa majesté
Dans cet enfant qui naît,
A son aspect qui plaît,
Je découvre mon maître
Et je sens ce qu'il est
Sans le connaître.

Here in this sta-ble Lies beauty, rich and rare; The precious Jesus, A-based, and yet so

1 Dans cette é-ta-ble Que Jé-sus est charmant, Qu'il est ai-ma-ble Dans cet a-bais-se
2 Que sa puis-san-ce Pa-raît bien en ce jour, Mal-gré l'en-fan-ce Où l'a ré-duit la-

Cresc ----

fair. What love-li-ness He brings! The pal-a-ces of kings Can-not compare in
ment! Que d'attraits à la fois! Tous les pa-lais des Rois N'ont rien de com-pa-
mour! Notre en-ne-mi domp-té, L'en-fer dé-con-cer-té, Font voir qu'en sa nais-

un poco rit.

gran-deur With all the love-ly things, Here in this sta- --ble
ra-ble Aux charmes que je vois Dans cette é- ta- -ble!
san-ce, Rien n'est si re-dou-té Que sa puis-san- --ce.

4
Plus de misère!
Un Dieu souffre pour nous
Et de son père
Appaise le courroux;
C'est en notre faveur
Qu'il naît dans la douleur;
Pouvait-il pour nous plaire
Unir à sa grandeur
Plus de misère!

Lo! Angel Bands
ANIELSKI CHÓR

Polish Text = JAN SIEDLECKI
English Version = FELICIAN SISTERS

Tyrolienne Air
Arranged = JAN SIEDLECKI

Lo! an-gel bands in still of night came down where shepherds lay To
A-niel-ski chór pa-ste — rzom o-gła-sza zbawie-nie, Zwia-

fill the dale with vi-sions bright and ti-dings glad to say: That
stu — jąc im bo-skie — go sło-wa wy-peł-nie-nie, Że

Christ is born of Ma — ry, the promised day has neared, The
w szop-ce z Pan-ny czy — stej, Zba-wca się na-ro-dził, By

dawn of hope and sav-ing grace has now at last ap-peared.
nas dzie-dzi-ców nie — ba, z więzow o-swo-bo-dził.

2 "Salvation" sang the angels loud to shepherds at their fold,
Tonight the Lord did send His Son, as prophets had foretold.
As He weeps in the manger so on the cross He'll die;
Through greatest love and sacrifice salvation will come nigh.

3 O sing, ye fearful shepherds, the "Gloria" from above,
Bring forth your gifts so humble with joy and greatest love.
The Child came down from heaven, for sinners far and near;
The silent Word is pleading: "Good Christians, do not fear."

2 W niedoli i ubóstwie Pan nieba przychodzi,
On tym cierpieniem nędzy wszystko nam osłodzi.
Jak leżąc płacze w żłóbku, tak i na krzyżu skona;
Wielkim cudem miłości odkupu dokona.

3 Nućcie więc wdzięczne pienia Dzieciątku pasterze,
Nieście Mu wasze dary w uprzejmej ofierze;
Z uśmiechem przyjmie miłym. On z nocnych nas ciemności
Wywiedzie na dzień jasny w niebieskie światłości.

Little Boy Down the Lane

BY GRACE NOLL CROWELL

Illustrated by Lee Mero

WHEN Noel John Peter Henry Williams was born it was a very stormy Christmas day, but such a good time for any little child to come to earth, to share, as it were, the great hour with the Christ Child.

And it was his father, bending above the golden-haired mother with the babe in her arms, who said in a great, booming voice, "Alice, I would like it well to call him Noel, for the good day on which he is born, and John for my father, and it would make me proud for him to bear my own two names, Peter and Henry." And although it seemed to the mother far too many names for such a little one, she was too tired to say other than, "Yes, Peter," as she smiled wanly to show that she was glad.

However, the names did not prove too heavy a load for the child to bear, for he became plump and strong, and grew to be a fine, upstanding lad.

But alas, the father, who loved him much, before little Noel John Peter Henry had come to know him as his father, went out one day with his fishing boat to the great waters, and a wild storm took him, leaving the little mother a widow, the child fatherless.

The small house in which they lived remained the same: a little gray house down a gray, crooked lane. At least in the autumn light they were gray and colorless; but one could view far off the shine of the sea, and one could smell it if the wind came right, and there were rock-strewn meadows near by where small boys could play. In the winter, after the great snows, the lane looked for all the world like a beautiful, sparkling Christmas card, and the little house as if hands had placed a fluffy angora hood upon its head and had tied it snugly under its chin, leaving only the two shining windows for eyes with which to look out upon the transformed and lovely world.

59

As little Noel grew older his mother could only manage one name for him, for so active was he, and so many times must she speak to him, to teach him, to chide him, to love him, and while all the names were kept as golden links in memory of the beloved lost father, yet he had become simply "little Noel" to the busy mother.

Always Noel was pleased that his birthday was the same as the Christ Child's. He was glad to share his day thus, and he ever had a pleased secret feeling that he and the Child had something wonderful in common which they could speak of often together. Christmas meant more to him than to anyone else, he knew, for had he not the name that meant Christmas time? And did not his mother make a special occasion of the day, reading often from the Good Book they kept on the center table under the hanging lamp that gave such a rosy light? She would read of the first Christmas; of the worshipping shepherds, and of the three Kings who came riding high on their huge, rocking camels, and bearing their glittering gifts for the Messiah who had come to earth at last after the long waiting.

Noel had fancied he could see them there, the dark forms of the camels black against the desert night sky, the men sitting tall and straight upon their hump-backed beasts, their eyes burning into the night as they sought to follow the star far off at the desert's rim. He felt sure he could see the bright star over neighbor Martin's house moving along like a silver lamp, slowly and silently, and he wished he might be one to follow it. He had even learned to roll the strange, traditional, rich-sounding names of the three Kings from his tongue and was pleased that he could do so. "Melchior, Caspar, Balthasar," he would repeat, smiling up at his mother, and she would smile back and say, "Such great words for so small a boy!"

He liked much the sound the words made as they fell from his lips, and he would repeat them over and over, savoring their fine flavor. He even felt he knew which king carried the gold, and which the frankincense and which the myrrh. Almost little Noel fancied he could see the saddle bags overflowing with gorgeous jewels: red and purple and green stones set deep in their splendid gold mountings. He was certain he could smell the clean scent of the frankincense, and the bitter tang of the myrrh. He thought the myrrh must be like the clear amber of the gum on the wild cherry tree in the meadow yonder. The frankincense with its sweet scent he felt sure would be poured into bright cut-glass bottles that sparkled magnificently.

Oh, they were gorgeous treasures the wise men were bringing across the desert to the Christ Child! The boy longed to feel the jewels—to lift them and see them dripping through his fingers. Their light and color would take his breath away, he knew, for they would be so very beautiful!

That evening, the night before Christmas Eve, his mother had taken down the Good Book and was again reading aloud to him as he sat upon the hassock at her feet before the crackling hearth fire. He liked the look of the smooth yellow braids wrapped neatly about her head. Despite the years of widowhood and poverty, her hair was still as golden as a finch's wing, and tonight with the firelight playing upon it, Noel kept remembering those flashing birds of the summertime.

"My mother is very beautiful," he thought. He especially liked the looks of her hands. They were such able hands! He liked to watch them doing things quietly and well. How quickly they moved among the bright yarns when they shaped his scarlet mittens, her knitting needles flashing like the silver of the far-off sea. Those hands could scrub the rough boards of their cottage floor until the grain came out in the old wood like water rippling over the pond when the wind scurried across it; they could feed the squealing pig in the sty, and they could scatter the golden grain to the cackling hens in the yard; but best of all they could soothe little Noel's forehead when he was ill, until he would think they were like feathers touching him, so full of love and tenderness were her hands.

Tonight they opened the Book at the story of the Christ Child's coming. Such quiet hands they were now, like a dove's wings folded down as she read of the great star shining silverly upon the stable—a sta-

ble, no doubt, such as their own with the animals all about.

But ever in Noel's mind there was the beauty of the gifts the Christ Child was about to receive. He could see the rubies glowing red in the starlight; the emeralds, sparkling like the green meadow with the dew upon it. The purple jewels would be like his mother's flags that blossomed in April along the front walk. He would turn the colors over and over in his mind as one turns a kaleidoscope, and he could almost hear the faint clinking they made, and he could see them glittering there.

He liked to imagine the sweet flower scent that the frankincense would give forth from the crystal bottles. Yet he always felt quite sad not having any gift whatsoever for the birthday of the Christ Child. He longed with a great longing for some rich and shining jewel that he might take and lay down at the manger side for the Child's eager, reaching hands to clasp and hold. If he only had one single gold bead, or a bit of amber-colored scent which he himself had crushed from the petals of the yellow roses that blossomed so warmly beside the little wicket gate in the summertime, how glad he would be! Surely, he thought, nothing but yellow roses could make that golden fragrance. Nothing else could make one want to breathe and breathe it until one drew all the sweetness into one's body to hold it there.

Noel knew there was no gift at all for him to bring to the Christ Child. The brown clay crock on the clock's shelf held not one single silver coin, nor would there be any until the day the pension came.

"O Mother," he cried at last, "I wish very much I could take a gift to the Christ Child! I wish I could!"

The dear mother-hands went out to him at once with the feel of wings about them. "I know, little Noel, but if you will be a good boy you will be giving Him the best gift of all. He will like it much better than silver or gold, my son."

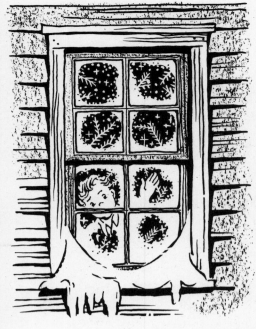

The next morning—Christmas Eve morning—dawned beautifully clear and sparkling. The little wicket gate with its burden of snow looked twice its size. It twinkled back at Noel as he stood at the window peering out through the spot he had melted among the frost flowers there.

The little crooked lane all but called out to him to come and try its unbroken whiteness.

There is something about Christmas Eve day that is like sparks flying upward. You cannot really see them, yet they are there, leaping in your heart every which way, and what boy could keep still with his heart on fire with gladness? Surely not little Noel Williams!

He must hurry and get into the wooly coat his mother had made snug and warm from the wool of their own white sheep. He must find his mittens. . . .

His mother was out in the barn getting the milk for their breakfast from old Bossy. He must wait until she came in.

Just then, from between the fern leaves on the pane, Noel saw small Joe, the new neighbor boy who had recently come to live in the most shabby of all the lane houses. He was struggling through the deep snow, a wobbly basket knocking against his knees, and he was crying as if his little heart would break.

Noel flung on his coat and cap, and pulled his mittens on as he ran out to the gate. "Joe, what is the matter with you? What has happened?" he inquired gravely. "Just why are you crying?"

Joe shaped his mouth into a big letter O and howled harder than ever.

"Little Joe, you must tell me. Why are you crying?" Noel demanded quite severely now.

"They hurt! My hands hurt! Mother sent me to the village to get milk for our baby, and my hands hurt!" Again the cry lifted to the far blue winter sky.

"You come into my house by the fire. You can get good and warm there, and I shall give you my mittens to wear. See—here they are," and Noel took the basket from the benumbed hands and guided the sobbing boy into the cheer and warmth of the red-lit kitchen.

"There now—you must get warm. Your hands will not get cold when you go home, for you will have my mittens to wear, and see, here is Mother with the milk. You will not have to go to the village for milk for your baby."

Joe wiped a very red nose with the red mittens and straightened beneath the comforting warmth of the fire.

The mother smiled happily at the two boys. "And how is your mother, Joe? And how is the baby? Indeed you must have Noel's mittens, for you will need them when you go out of doors to work or to play. Keep them for your own, Joe." She turned and filled the small milk bottles in the basket with the warm, foaming milk. She gave Joe and Noel each a cupful to drink, and a brown rusk to eat, and the boy went on his way, warmed and comforted.

"He was crying much, Mother, and I was very sorry for him," Noel explained. "You do not mind that I gave him my mittens?" he questioned.

"No, that was good, little Noel. I am glad you gave them to him. I shall make others for you, and poor little Joe would have had frozen fingers had you not brought him in and made him warm."

Noel turned to his mother: "May I go to see Grandma Parker this morning, Mother? I think she may be needing some sticks for her fire. I could get them for her."

"Yes, Child, but you must wear my mittens or soon you, too, will be crying like little Joe, and you must button your coat well."

So Noel went trudging out across the fields toward the little house where Grandma Parker lived. The snow was very deep and he looked much like a snow man as he struggled through its glittering whiteness. He could see her house with its low eaves barely lifting above the white drifts.

Grandma Parker was very old and she was almost bent double with rheumatism. Why she was called Grandma, Noel didn't know, but all the children along the lane spoke of her thus. Perhaps it was because she was stooped and wrinkled and toothless; yet her heart was as good and sound as a red apple on a summer orchard tree, and Noel liked to go to her house and hear the strange tales of the sea which her father, and his fathers before him, had sailed in the old days.

Noel always knew that some day he, too, would be a man of the sea, as his forefathers had been, and so he and Grandma Parker had much to say to one another, and often it took long to say it, so that the mother at home wondered what was keeping the boy.

there, and now, so pleased was she to see little Noel on this fine winter morning, she arose with much difficulty, plumped up the chair pillows, and taking him gently by the shoulders she pushed him snugly down among the feathers that went "poof" as he sat on them. Then with her old gnarled hands she stooped and placed his numbed feet on the little box stove.

"There now," she said in her queer manner, "that is good after the cold walk, not?"

He found the old woman sitting, as she almost always did, in a huge wooden rocking chair which was made soft and puffy with many feather cushions. To be sure, they squashed down as she sat upon them, but they puffed up between the slats of the rocker and billowed out at the back. In the winter, to keep her feet warm, she used a foot-warmer: a small wooden box it was, with holes bored in the top, and inside of it there was an iron pan in which she placed live coals from her kitchen stove. The coals would glow redly

Indeed, Noel thought it was much better: such a soft, nice seat—such warmth for his tingling toes!

After he was thoroughly warmed he went out to gather the sticks for the all-but-empty wood box. He scraped the snow from the small wood pile. He gathered an old stump here, a fallen branch of a tree there, which must be broken. Then there was the basket of coal to be brought in for the little foot stove.

When he had finished at last and the box behind the stove was overflowing with fuel, Grandma Parker was so pleased she clapped her crooked hands glee-fully together and said, "You wait now, little Noel, and see the fine Christmas gift I have for you."

She rose stiffly and hobbled into the low side bed-room, and came out immediately with the most aston-ishing gift indeed! It was an old silver-handled knife which had a wide-winged sailing ship carved deeply upon the handle, and the steel blade was as sharp and bright as the winter wind.

"This is a knife," she said, "that belonged to my father and to his father, and to his father's father a long time ago. It is very precious, and some day, little Noel, you may sell it and get much money."

"Oh, no, no, Grandma Parker!" Noel was quick to exclaim, "I shall always keep it. I shall never part with it! I shall use it to make the kindling for Mother, and some day I shall carve a ship like the one on the handle, from a piece of our wood, and then it may be I, too, will carry it to sea. But now I must go or my mother will be thinking I stay too long." And the boy started home with his heart as light as the feathers in Grandma Parker's chair pillows, not only because of the shining gift he had received, which he was eager to show to his mother, but because the wood and coal were ready for his old friend to burn and keep warm by, not only her crooked body, but her poor crippled feet.

As he crossed the stile into the little lane he saw the Martin dog coming toward him, limping pain-fully. Noel stopped and called to him. The dog whined piteously and came slowly toward the boy.

"Come, dog, let me see what is hurting you," Noel called, and the dog came, holding up his paw trust-ingly. Indeed, there was reason for that limping. A thorn from the haw tree branch yonder had pierced the soft, pad-like foot deeply. Little Noel had to pull with all his might to remove it, but finally, out it came, leaving a trickle of blood on the snow.

In his relief the dog licked the boy's hands with his great, splashing tongue. He licked the injured paw, then turned and trotted home across the white mead-ow, his tail wagging in expressive gladness.

Noel went on scanning the winter landscape. He came upon a cluster of snow birds that were picking at the foodless snow. They were jigging away on their wire-like legs like the dancer Noel had once seen in the village. They looked so funny to him that he had to laugh. Then he thought how cold they must be, and how hungry!

Such thin, bloodless legs and feet with no shoes and stockings to keep them warm! It may be, Noel thought, they are really not so cold as they seem, for he recalled having heard his mother tell of some places where there were power houses that sent light and heat into far-away homes, and perhaps God, who loved the birds much, had made their little fast-beat-ing hearts like power houses that could send warmth into the wire-like legs and claws to keep them from freezing on cold winter days. Noel hoped very much that this might be so.

He had thought of another thing his mother had told him. She said they had a custom in another coun-try where children, grateful for their own food on Christmas day, would tie sheaves of wheat onto the fence posts for the birds to find and enjoy. He must remember to go to Bossy's stall and say: "Please, may I have this sheaf, Bossy? I want it for the little hungry birds that can find no food," and Bossy, he knew, would say, "Moo," which in cow language would mean "Yes," and he would bring the sheaf to the low fence post yonder, that the birds might have their food.

Suddenly Noel heard a strange, muffled sound in the nearby thicket. It frightened him for a moment. Then came a faint bleat as he peered through the tangled bushes.

He saw that it was neighbor Robinson's old fat sheep that had become caught in the brambles. Noel was glad he had his good sharp knife. He would use it to free the tired old sheep. He worked away dili-gently, scratching his face and pricking his hands, but at last the clumsy sheep gave a bleat and a leap and was off and away.

"I think it was because she was so old that she could not free herself," Noel reflected as he turned into his own gate at last, tired from his varied experi-ences, yet happy even so for the lovely morning. He showed his mother the wonderful gift Grandma Parker had given him; he told of his small adventures, and that evening again—Christmas Eve at last—his mother read again the Christmas story to the child.

Noel sat with his chin cupped in his hands, the fire-light playing over his fair cheeks and wheat-colored hair. At last he sighed deeply: "Mother, now it is Christmas Eve and I have no gift for the Christ Child —not a jewel or a sweet scent—I have nothing at all."

And the mother, her nice hands again reaching out in understanding love, answered softly:

"Little son, all day, without your knowing it, you have been bringing gifts to the Christ which have made Him very glad."

"But Mother, I brought nothing. I would give Him my silver knife—I would, if I could only find Him. . . ."

And the mother answered: "You have given Him more than jewels or a sweet scent, or the silver knife, Noel. When the Christ Child had grown to be a man He said many wise things to those who were gathered about Him. Once He said: 'I was a stranger and ye took me in.' Early this morning you took the stranger boy, Joe, into your house. You warmed him and comforted him. Do you not see you were doing it for the Christ? And that same time He said: 'Inasmuch as ye have done it unto one of the least of these, ye have done it unto me.' Surely little Joe was very small and needy this morning when you brought him in, and the birds are among the least of God's creatures.

"Christ was ever mindful of the birds," she went on. "Do you not recall what we read together of the sparrows? 'Not one falls,' we are told, 'without the Father seeing it.' I am sure He was much pleased when you brought the grain for His hungry birds. And little Noel, there is much in the Good Book about sheep. The Christ told of the one lost sheep that had wandered far, and all night long the good shepherd went seeking for it, when many were left in the fold. So, little Noel, when you set the poor, tired sheep free from the thicket today, you were doing what Christ would have done. Do you not see?

"Then you fetched the wood for neighbor Parker, and made her glad. The Christ said, 'I was sick and ye visited me'—and Grandma Parker is far from well —so you really were visiting the Christ today, little Noel, although you did not know it. The Christ's heart, too, would have yearned over the dog with the hurt paw. He would have stopped as you did, and He, too, would have healed the hurt. You have been a workman with Him this day, little Noel."

The boy looked up with wide, wondering eyes at his mother, not able to comprehend at first. "But Mother, I did not have a real gift. I am glad you think I brought good gifts to Him, and if I only thought that one of them might shine before Him like a jewel, and one might have a sweet scent like the gifts of the three Kings, I would be most glad."

And the mother smiled and said: "I am sure they all shine brightly, and I think there is a sweet scent upon the air tonight rising up to Him—a very sweet odor."

Noel, tired from the long, exciting day, nodded sleepily. "And I did not know they were gifts at all. I thought it was just living."

"Just living as the Christ would have you do, little Noel. That is the best gift of all to bring Him."

66

OPPOSITE PAGE

Canadian Winter
by Garnet Hazard

Twentieth Century Y's Men

BY MELVA ROREM

CHRISTMAS seemed to be everywhere, Jim thought as he edged closer to the lot where Christmas trees were being sold. He could see it in the crowded streets as folks hurried on their way past the lot. He could see it in the new snow that fell softly on the spruce and pine and fir and hemlock, and in the happy faces of families that came to choose *their* tree. (It was almost something of a ceremony, this deciding which tree was the one for them.) He could feel it in the kind voices that called "Merry Christmas" to him, and in the warm smiles in eyes that met his. He could hear it in the carols played at intervals throughout the day that sang themselves into the hearts of everyone as their song was carried by a loud speaker to every corner of the lot.

It would take some sort of miracle, like Christmas, Jim thought, for business and professional men to take long hours from their busy before-Christmas-days, selling trees at lots such as this in order to help boys who couldn't otherwise afford it, go to summer camp. He dared to hope that he would be one of those chosen when summer came again! And suddenly the fragrance of spruce was tangled in his dreams with the aroma of food cooked over an open fire. And the gay lilt of Christmas carols blended with a bugle's clear, commanding call. . . .

Such dreams as Jim's have come true for thousands of American boys because of another dream born in the heart of Mr. John Werness, a young Minneapolis business man. In 1938, when elected president of the only Y's Men's Club in Minneapolis (which now has nine such clubs), he proposed the idea that his club sell Christmas trees, using the profits to send underprivileged boys to YMCA summer camps. Their treasury was then in the red, and without funds it was impossible to render such a service to their community.

The first year the idea was tried the club made a substantial profit, but not because it was an idea that operated by

some sort of magic. It worked because Mr. Werness knew that such a dream was worth all the long hours of work he must put behind it. It meant such practical things as investing his own money in the venture. It meant the tediousness of hours and hours, long before December came, spent organizing his group for action. It meant the effort of instilling in the hearts of other club members, zealousness for a cause in which he believed. It meant meeting truckers who arrived with shipments of trees that must be unloaded in early morning hours, and then going home to snatch an hour or two of sleep before being at his office at the usual hour. It meant sparing no effort, because the dream must come true. And it did.

Y's MEN'S CLUB
CHRISTMAS TREES
Proceeds for Children's Summer Camps

and from one to over four hundred clubs in twenty-seven countries on six continents. The founder and first president of the International Association of Y's Men's Clubs is Judge Paul W. Alexander, of Toledo, Ohio.

Christmas tree selling, and what it has meant in the lives of many boys, is only one phase, of course, of the work they have done as service clubs of the YMCA. But the results of this contribution alone are immeasurable. And Y's Men are assured that possibilities for Christmases to come are boundless.

In Minneapolis, six tree lots are operated now by Y's Men. A few years ago the space they used to initiate their venture at the corner of 46th Street and Lyndale Avenue, was going to be sold. Rather than lose a location familiar to their Christmas tree buyers for nine years, two members of the club bought the house and two lots to hold until proper club financing could be arranged. When a project is supported by such openhearted loyalty it cannot fail. To visit a Y's Men's Christmas tree lot and observe these men lost in work they are doing for others is to have the heart lifted to new and inspiring heights.

A Y's Man is a young man between the ages of twenty and thirty-six. He is not elected to the club if

Today, nearly two hundred Y's Men's Clubs throughout our country sell Christmas trees. "Is there a boy in *your* Christmas tree?" they ask their fellow citizens wherever trees are sold.

During the past quarter-century, Y's Men's Clubs have been organized throughout the world—from Sydney, Nova Scotia, to Sydney, Australia; from China to Czechoslovakia. In that time the organization has grown from seventeen to eleven thousand members,

fellow members suspect that he is interested in what he can get out of it for himself. He is elected because he asks for the high privilege of putting all that he has into it. Nor is he the ineffectual sort who *has* time on his hands. He *takes* time out of days that are already busy. Y's Men have been known to provide men to work in their offices during busy Christmas seasons, rather than hire substitutes to do their job at the tree lot. Each member tries to spend forty hours at the lot during the month. Those in charge of organizing their clubs for tree-selling give much more time.

Y's Menettes, an auxiliary club whose members are Y's Men's wives, serve coffee and doughnuts to their Y's Men every afternoon and evening at the lots. They are paid for this work and the money is used to send underprivileged girls to camp.

Hi-Y boys help, too. In the experimental days of the project Mr. Werness asked his friend, Mr. Stott, if his son Jack might help by tying trees on purchasers' cars. Jack agreed to help. And today Hi-Y boys from the east coast to the west are hired for this work and the money they earn is given to their clubs. "Hi, Jack!" the voices of Y's Men call out to these red capped boys, for it has become traditional for all of them to answer to the name of Jack, "another tree sold. . . ." And "Jack" gladly hurries to answer the call. He has caught the spirit of the Y's Men.

Teachers, pastors, and others who work with young people help Y's Men select boys who ought to know the joys and benefits of two weeks at camp. Boy Scout and church camps are used in instances where they seem to fit the needs of a particular child. But whatever the camp, boys of all creeds and all races and all nationalities have become stronger in body and mind and soul because a dream was born in the heart of a Y's Man twelve years ago.

The crowd was thinning out now, Jim noticed, but the music of Christmas was still ringing through the night air. Clear, confident voices sang out—

> . . . Yet in thy dark streets shineth
> The everlasting Light . . . .

His own street was dark, Jim mused. Dark with poverty and want and loneliness. But Y's Men were near. And like Wise men from the East of long ago they were following a Star and seeking a Child. For they, too, worshipped Him with gifts of gold, and frankincense, and myrrh. Their gold . . . the golden laughter of a boy. Their frankincense . . . glad hearts that worshipped Him. Their myrrh . . . the sacrificial gifts of time and love—that the Everlasting Light might shine again in darkened streets.

Volume I - 1931

Volume II - 1932

Volume III - 1933

Volume IV - 1934

Volume V - 1935

Volume VI - 1936

Volume VII - 1937

Volume VIII - 1938

Volume IX - 1939

Volume X - 1940

Volume XI - 1941

Volume XII - 1942

Volume XIII - 1943

Volume XIV - 1944

Volume XV - 1945

Volume XVI - 1946

Volume XVII - 1947

Volume XVIII - 1948

Volume XIX - 1949

Under the direction of Randolph E. Haugan, writers, artists, and craftsmen have created and put into tangible form the material that makes up this twentieth volume of CHRISTMAS. The text is set in Caledonia Type and the headings are in Goudy Blackletter with Lombardic Capitals. Augsburg Publishing House in Minneapolis printed the volume by the Photo-offset Lithographic Process.